Look How
Many People Wear
Glasses

The Magic of Lenses

Look How Many People Wear Glasses

The Magic of Lenses

RUTH BRINDZE

ILLUSTRATED BY PHOTOGRAPHS

AND DRAWINGS

A MARGARET K. MCELDERRY BOOK

Atheneum 1979 *New York*

*Jacket photographs by Edward Stevenson and
Better Vision Institute*

Library of Congress Cataloging in Publication Data

Brindze, Ruth.
  Look how many people wear glasses.

  "A Margaret K. McElderry book."
  SUMMARY: Traces the history of spectacles over seven
hundred years and discusses how lenses are made, how
eyes work, and how to choose the right glasses.
  1. Lenses—Juvenile literature. 2. Eyeglasses—Juvenile
literature. [1. Lenses. 2. Eyeglasses]
                    I. Title.
      QC385.B67   617.7'522   75-8947
            ISBN 0-689-50028-9

Contents

Look How
Many People Wear
Glasses

The Magic of Lenses

One of Every Two Americans Wears Eyeglasses

According to a recent survey made by the U.S. Public Health Service, nearly one of every two Americans over the age of three wears spectacles. In addition, some people with vision defects use contact lenses, small discs that are placed directly on the eyes and are invisible.

If the results of the official survey surprise you, look at your classmates or at any other group of people and you will see how widespread is the use of spectacles. Yet experts say that even more people need eyeglasses than wear them.

The figures compiled by the Health Service show that more girls than boys wear glasses. In the 3 to 16 age group, bespectacled girls outnumbered bespectacled boys by 22 percent. The differential increased to about 50 percent for the 17 to 24 age group. The survey includes statistics for five groups, the last being 65 and over, and in all the groups the figures for females who wear glasses exceed those for males.

So common is the use of spectacles that most people take them for granted. This is a mistake. When you first look through a microscope, a telescope or a pair of binoculars (all three invented hundreds of years ago by eyeglass makers), you are thrilled by what these instruments enable you to see. Spectacles are equally remarkable optical devices.

The history of eyeglasses is intriguing. Who invented them and when remains a mystery, although many people have tried to solve it. The first record describing an eyeglass is dated 1268. In that year the famous English scientist, Roger Bacon, wrote that even small letters could be read by people with weak eyes by looking through a glass "shaped like the lesser segment of a sphere, with the convex [rounded] side towards the eye."

The magnifying lens led to the development of spectacles. At first few people used them. Until Johann Gutenberg invented the printing press, most people were illiterate and eye defects, especially farsightedness, caused little difficulty. This state of affairs gradually changed after printed books became available. As the number of readers increased, and as people discovered how greatly vision is improved by eyeglasses, the demand for them grew.

There came a time when it was fashionable to use eyeglasses. In a book entitled *The Ingenious and Diverting Letters of a Lady*, Maria de Berneville, Countess d'Aulnoy, included the following about her visit to Madrid in 1679.

"I was surprised to see many young ladies with great spectacles on their noses and fastened to their ears. But what seemed strangest to me was that they made no use of them where it was necessary; they only discoursed while they had them on. I was told that it was done to make them look serious. They did not wear them for necessity but to draw respect."

The Countess then commented on the use of spectacles by men. She wrote: "It is so common a thing to wear them that I

This engraving showing a man selecting a pair of spectacles is a reproduction of a painting completed in 1600. Notice that the men and women in the picture are wearing spectacles and one man is holding a single lens to his eye.

Courtesy of the New York Public Library.

understand there are different spectacles according to rank. As a man increases the size of his fortune, he increases the size of his lenses. The grandees of Spain wear them as broad as one's hand."

Wealthy women who needed spectacles (and some who did not) wore folding spectacles on a chain around their neck when they went to balls or attended other social events. Many lorgnettes, as the folding spectacles were called, had elaborately engraved gold or silver frames. Lorgnettes were neither convenient to use nor really comfortable. After they were snapped open they were clipped on the nose or held by a handle. Opening a pair of lorgnettes was done with a flourish intended to attract attention.

Men wore monocles generally as show-off accessories. A monocle is a single eyeglass: the first ones were held by a handle but the monocles used by fashionable men were held on the face in front of the right or left eye by the muscles that control the opening and closing of eyelids. Mastering the trick of holding a monocle in place required practice. However, if a monocle fell out there was no danger that it would be broken because it was attached to a ribbon or cord worn around the neck. Gentlemen wore monocles while they conversed or danced, but even though some monocles contained corrective lenses they usually were not worn for reading. When a man with defective vision sat down to read he removed his monocle and put on spectacles.

Today, most spectacles are designed to be both practical and attractive but there still are faddish ones, as for example, the large round frames that some girls favor. Large ones, like those of average size, should be fitted so that they are correctly lined up with the eyes. When oversized spectacles are worn near the tip of the nose, as frequently they are, the lenses can do little to correct defective eyesight.

We have come a long way since spectacles were sold ready-made and a buyer had to judge for himself which pair was best for him. Now each pair of corrective eyeglasses is made for one individual. The lenses conform to the prescription of the doctor who examined the patient's eyes. The two lenses in the spectacles may not be identical. Frequently the right and left eyes do

Pamela P. Franklin who starred in the movie, The Prime of Miss Jean Brodie, *wears large round spectacles, not as a visual aid, but as a fashion accessory.*

not have the same defects. Sometimes only one eye requires a corrective lens. In such cases a lens without optical power, known as a plano lens, is used for the normal eye.

The manufacture of optical glass is a specialized and highly technical process. As a matter of fact, until World War I the United States depended for optical glass on European producers. The imported glass was used not only for eyeglasses but also for lenses for cameras, microscopes and telescopes.

Most spectacle lenses are made of what is called crown glass. It is similar in composition to plate glass used for windows but is more highly refined. Imperfections that are of no importance in plate glass make optical glass worthless. If it contains a tiny bubble or vein, less than the width of a hair, the glass cannot be used for spectacle lenses. It may seem to be a simple discovery that bubbles can be eliminated by mixing glass while it is in the melted state with a stirrer made of fireclay, but for a long time this method was the secret of the man who devised it. In modern optical glass factories the stirring is done mechanically in the furnaces in which glass is made.

Scientists have had a key role in the manufacture of optical glass. Experiments have not only led to improvements in the quality of optical glass but also to the development of many different types with special characteristics. Only after a long series of experiments with coloring materials was a formula developed for making glass a neutral gray, the most efficient color for sunglasses. Experiments also showed the percentage of lead to add to the glass mix to increase the power of a lens to bend light and to make the glass easy to fuse. Both of these characteristics are important in the production of a bifocal (two focus) lens. The lower section of such a lens is used for reading or other close work and the upper section for distance vision. Since lenses made of lead glass have some disadvantages, scientists continued to test other materials. They were successful when they tried barium. Now, most bifocal lenses are made of barium glass.

Perhaps the chief reason why more people than ever before wear spectacles is because greater attention is being paid to eyes. More is known about the way eyes work and how to correct vision defects.

TWO

Seven Hundred Years of Spectacles

When Roger Bacon wrote about using a magnifying glass as an aid for weak eyes he did not know that spectacles had been developed in China. There was no way that he could have known about Chinese inventions or customs. The East was sealed off from the western world until Marco Polo returned from his travels in China, and he did not start to dictate his account of the land he called Kublai Khan until 1296. Bacon had described his reading glass nearly thirty years earlier in his book, *Opus Majus.* It was a scientific encyclopedia prepared at the request of Pope Clement IV, who previously had served as papal representative in England where he became acquainted with Bacon.

During Bacon's lifetime, a device that could correct a physical defect was classed as black magic. Because of his scientific activities Bacon was suspected of practicing black magic and later was condemned and sent to prison for two years for his work in alchemy and astrology. He was probably careful not to spread word about his knowledge of optics, and his only statement about the usefulness of an eyeglass was in the encyclopedia prepared with the encouragement of the Pope.

One historian has suggested and it is reasonable to believe, that Bacon started with a magnifying glass placed on the page he was reading and then found that it was better to hold the glass closer to his eye. Perhaps next he decided to use two glasses, one in front of each eye and thus invented spectacles.

Based on known facts, and filling in details, it appears that Heinrich Goethals, one of Bacon's friends, introduced eyeglasses into Italy. Goethals went there in 1285 to present a petition to the Pope, and although there is no actual proof that he carried eyeglasses with him, it seems likely that he did from subsequent developments.

Goethals stayed for some time at the monastery in Pisa where he met Brother Alessandro della Spina. According to the monastery's records, Alessandro "understood how to reproduce anything he saw and of which he had heard." After Goethals' visit, Alessandro proceeded to make eyeglasses which, the record says, he "distributed with a cheerful and benevolent heart." As a result he became known as the inventor of eyeglasses.

Credit for the invention was also given to Salvino d'Armati of Florence and his knowledge of eyeglasses can also be traced to Goethals. Travelers usually show the interesting things they have with them and while Goethals was in Florence he probably displayed his eyeglasses. Apparently Salvino was impressed and became a maker of eyeglasses. Whether Salvino said that spectacles were his idea is not known, but whoever wrote the inscription for his tombstone stated: "Here lies Salvino of the Armatis of Florence, inventor of spectacles. God pardon his sins."

In February 1306, Brother Giordana di Rivalto of Pisa mentioned spectacles in a sermon, saying, "It is not yet twenty years since the art of making spectacles, one of the most useful arts on earth, was discovered." The date given for the discovery was shortly after Goethals' arrival in Italy.

By the middle 1300s many churchmen used eyeglasses. A painting completed in 1352, which decorates a wall in a church in Treviso, Italy, portrays a group of men, including Cardinal Ugone who is wearing spectacles and Nicholas of Rouen who is holding a single eyeglass by a handle.

Painting of a churchman who lived in medieval times balancing riveted spectacles on his nose.

Courtesy of the New York Public Library.

When books were handwritten, few copies were made and most of them were owned by churches and universities. After books were printed and could be bought by anyone who had enough money, more people began to read. Reading disclosed eye defects that previously had not been noticed. People whose vision was adequate for other purposes could not see well enough to read. The solution for many people with eye defects was spectacles.

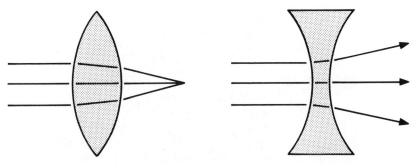

Light rays passing through a convex lens are bent together and form a clear image on the retina of the eye. Convex lenses are prescribed to correct farsightedness.
Light rays passing through a concave lens are bent apart. This form makes light rays from distant objects diverge with the result that the rays are correctly focused on the retina.

Courtesy of the Better Vision Institute.

The first were designed for people who were farsighted. This defect makes it difficult, or impossible, to see things that are close up. The lens Bacon describes in his encyclopedia was an aid for the farsighted. Its convex shape bent light rays from nearby things so that they converged and formed a clear image on the retina of the eye. Eyeglasses for nearsighted people were introduced early in the sixteenth century. These lenses were concave. This form makes light rays from distant objects diverge with the result that the rays are correctly focused on the retina. Leo X who was Pope from 1513 to 1521 was nearsighted and was enthusiastic about his spectacles with concave lenses. He wore his spectacles when hunting and said that they made his aim better than that of his companions who did not wear glasses.

As the use of eyeglasses increased, making spectacles became a profitable business and, like other craftsmen, spectaclemakers organized guilds to regulate the manufacture of eyeglasses. In 1629, when Charles I of England gave a charter to the Worshipful Company of Spectaclemakers of London, its stated purpose was "for the better order, rule and government of those using the Art and Mistry of Spectaclemaking."

Included in the records of the London guild are entries of the fines and other penalties imposed on members who failed to comply with the standards established by the guild. One man, listed as J. Clark, was fined three pounds "for selling three pairs of spectacles made of looking glass." In other words, the lenses were not made of optical glass but of ordinary glass. Another member who had previously been fined was expelled "for selling a great quantity of improper wares viz.: frames without glasses."

Spectaclemakers did not do all the manufacturing work themselves: they had apprentices whom they trained to make eyeglasses. The rules of the London guild fixed sixteen as the age at which an apprenticeship could be started and provided that an apprentice was to work nine years before being permitted to apply for membership in the guild. To be accepted, the applicant was required to submit samples of eyeglasses he had made to the guild's examining board. If it found the samples to be satisfactory, the applicant was awarded the title of master. As a

Fanciful portrait of a seventeenth-century peddler. His stock includes spectacles, single reading glasses, a telescope and varied jewelry.

master spectaclemaker he could open a shop and employ apprentices. Girls as well as boys could become apprentices. Clark, who had been fined in 1670, took his daughter, Lucretia, as an apprentice in 1692.

Although the manufacture of spectacles was regulated, it was largely a matter of luck for a buyer to get eyeglasses that were right for him. Spectacles were sold in the same way as other merchandise. Peddlars and shops carried a stock of ready-made spectacles, and customers selected the pair they thought was best for them. Until quite recently the importance of examining eyes and the prescribing of glasses on an individual basis was not recognized.

A letter sent in 1852 to a London spectaclemaker indicates the nonscientific attitude toward eyeglasses. The letter, written by Lord Buckinghamshire's secretary, requested the spectaclemaker to send "a pair of spectacles such as he thinks will suit a youth of sixteen years of age, who has never worn any, but is so shortsighted as to be obliged to hold his face close to his plate when he takes his meals. The spectacles are wanted for one of Lord Buckinghamshire's sons."

At the time, and long afterwards, it was the practice to sell spectacles according to the age of the person who was to use them. There were different lenses for different ages. When a person went to a shop to buy spectacles, he was sometimes asked his age or the eyeglass maker guessed it. In most instances the customer made the final selection after trying on spectacles, but he made his choice from the stock considered to be suitable for a person of his age.

The spectacle frames supplied for the sixteen-year-old boy were probably made of steel. In earlier times frames were made of horn, tortoise shell, leather or wood. Later brass was used and, sometimes, gold or silver.

No convenient method for keeping spectacles on the nose was devised for hundreds of years. The first eyeglasses, riveted or wired together had to be balanced on the nose or were held by a handle.

Much thought was given to the improvement of nose bridges. When they were made of bone, pliability was increased by cutting horizontal slits in the nose bridge. Four slits was considered to be the most desirable number. The change to semicircular shaped metal bridges improved their appearance but did nothing to make spectacles more convenient to wear. They slipped down, or off, the nose if the wearer changed the position of his head.

Leather frames were often made with long straps which were tied in back of the head. The straps held the spectacles in place but they interfered with hairdos. Since men, as well as women, wore wigs, the tie-on leather straps were awkward to wear and did not become popular.

Then, in 1728, Edward Scarlett, a London spectaclemaker, published an account of an improved type of frame he had invented. The improvement was the addition of sidepieces. They

El Greco's striking portrait of Cardinal Don Fernando Niño de Guevara wearing spectacles of the style popular in Spain during the sixteenth century. The spectacles are held in place by loops fastened around the ears.

Courtesy of the Metropolitan Museum of Art.
Bequest of Mrs. H. O. Havemeyer, 1929.
The H. O. Havemeyer Collection.

were only about four inches long and fitted snugly against the wearer's temples. The sidepieces, or temples, as they came to be called, were designed to be convenient for people who wore wigs. Later, temples were made longer and now some hook around the ears and others grip the head behind the ears.

The next important improvement in eyeglasses was made a little more than fifty years after the addition of temples, when Benjamin Franklin conceived the idea for what he called "double spectacles." His ingenius invention, now known as bifocals, is in common use today.

As people grow older they may need lenses of different power for reading and for distance vision. Benjamin Franklin had this problem and for some time carried two pairs of spectacles. This in itself was inconvenient, but he found it even more inconvenient to change from one pair of spectacles to the other. To eliminate the necessity of changing glasses Franklin invented bifocals. He had the lenses from his two pairs of glasses cut in half lengthwise and then the lower halves of the reading glasses were cemented to the upper halves of the distance glasses. The cemented lenses were fitted into one of Franklin's spectacle frames. He was completely satisfied when he tried his combination eyeglasses. In a letter to a friend, Franklin described what he had done and said, "By this means, as I wear my spectacles constantly, I have only to move my eyes up or down as I want to see distinctly far or near, the proper glasses being always ready."

Franklin's double glasses looked cracked across the center and were crude compared to the bifocals manufactured today. Now the size and shape of the two segments is determined according to the use to which the spectacles are to be put.

*Benjamin Franklin invented bifocal (two focus) lenses by having
the upper half of his distance lenses and the lower half of his reading lenses cemented together and fitted into one frame.*
From Bausch & Lomb. Courtesy New York Public Library.

Usually the reading segment is comparatively small, but it
would be larger in glasses made for a librarian than in those
made for a bus driver who uses his eyes more for seeing at a distance than closeup. The two segments are joined by fusing and
the joining is inconspicuous.

Although bifocals are more frequently used by older people, they are occasionally prescribed for boys and girls whose
eye defects cannot be corrected by single lenses. Bifocals are

also prescribed in some special situations. For example, a thirteen-year-old boy who had worn glasses for several years was told, when his eyes were reexamined, that he no longer needed glasses for reading, but that he did need corrective lenses for distance vision. The doctor explained to the boy and his mother that he could prescribe glasses to be worn only for distance. "To see what is written on the blackboard you'd put on your glasses," said the doctor, "but I think you may find it such a nuisance to put on your glasses to see the blackboard and take them off for desk work that you may not use the glasses at all. I am therefore prescribing bifocal lenses, plano (without optical power) in the lower segment and corrective in the rest of the lens area. You'll be comfortable wearing these spectacles at all times."

THREE

How Your Eyes Work

The way eyes work—the way they receive and form images—is complicated and wonderful.

Human eyes are often compared to a camera, but no camera yet invented can equal what our eyes do. They not only adjust automatically for changes in light and for seeing things close up and at a distance, but they produce three dimensional movies or single pictures in full color or in black and white.

Before scientists figured out how human eyes function, many weird explanations were given. One was that sight depended on light rays projected by the eyes. Actually light rays enter the eyes. Light rays from a natural or artificial source that have bounced off the page of a book, a sign on a bus, a tree or whatever you are looking at are reflected into your eyes. Light rays enable us to see.

When light rays enter the eyes they are bent, or refracted. This is the first of a complex series of automatic processes that occur in the eyes and in the brain. The focusing parts of each eye form separate images on its light sensitive screen known as the retina. It is the innermost coat of the eyeball. Millions of cells in each retina send a description of the images to the sight center of the brain. The brain combines the signals transmitted by the sensory cells in the two retinas and translates them into a single understandable picture. Images are focused upside down on the retinas. As part of the translation process the brain turns the images right side up. All this is happening as you read this book.

Before light rays reach the retina they pass through a number of components of the eye, the first of which is called the cornea. It is the window of the eye. If you look in a mirror and examine the surfaces of your eyes you will be able to locate, but not to see, the corneas which are important parts of the focusing system. Corneas are transparent but can be identified because they bulge slightly. The eveness of the bulge affects the sharpness with which eyes focus.

One question that still puzzles scientists is how the cornea tissue is nourished since it has no blood supply. At present it is believed that nourishment is derived from the salts, sugar and other food substances in tears. They also contain the antiseptic, lysozyme. Corneas are always covered by a thin film of tears.

The white of the eye, through which light does not pass, is the visible part of the membrane called the sclera. This protective coat encloses about five-sixths of the eyeball, the other sixth is covered by the cornea. The sclera contains blood vessels which supply nourishment to the inner parts of the eye.

The colored iris is visible through the cornea. However, between the cornea and the iris there is a space filled with a fluid known by the Latin words *aqueous humor*, which mean watery liquid. It is similar in composition to tears. The aqueous helps to nourish the eye and to carry away waste products. The pressure exerted by the fluid is important in maintaining the curvature of the cornea. If, as a result of an accident, aqueous humor is lost, it is replaced by cells within the eye.

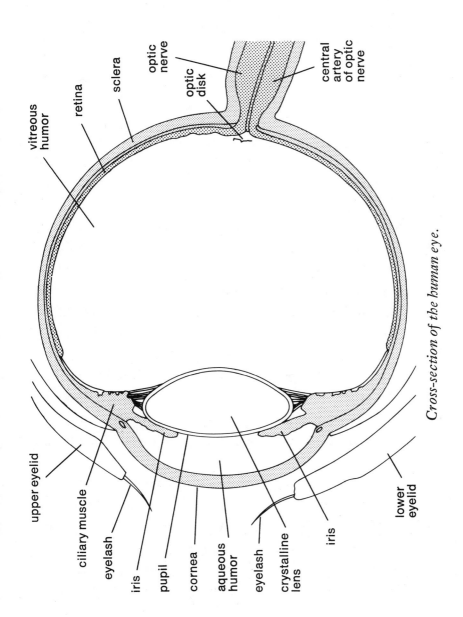

vitreous humor

retina

sclera

optic nerve

optic disk

central artery of optic nerve

upper eyelid

ciliary muscle

eyelash

iris

pupil

cornea

aqueous humor

eyelash

crystalline lens

iris

lower eyelid

Cross-section of the human eye.

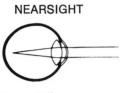

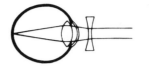
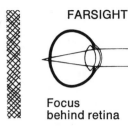

Focus falls
short of retina

Concave lens
gives correct focus

Focus
behind retina

The amount of coloring matter in the iris makes it look brown, blue, gray or hazel. Irises that contain lesser quantities of pigmentation are light in color; irises that are heavily pigmented are brown. Inheritance determines the color of eyes. If both parents have brown eyes, it is almost a certainty that their children will have brown eyes.

The iris is ring shaped, and its function is to regulate the size of the hole in its center through which light passes into the eye. The hole is called the pupil. When the light is bright the iris expands and the pupil contracts; when the light is dim the iris contracts and the pupil expands. What our eyes do automatically many photographers do manually when, before snapping a picture, they measure the light with a meter and then set the lens opening of their camera for the intensity of the light. They use a small opening for bright light and a large opening for dim light.

The lens of the eye, technically known as the crystalline lens because like a crystal it is clear, is suspended behind the iris. The lens is about the size of an aspirin tablet and is biconvex, that is, it is rounded both in front and in back. The front surface of the lens is more highly curved than the back. The transparent elastic capsule that encloses the lens is connected to muscles attached to the wall of the eyeball. These muscles change the shape of the lens for far and near vision. If you are

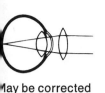

ASTIGMATISM

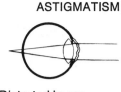

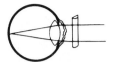

May be corrected
y convex lens

Distorted image
from irregular cornea

Cylindrical lens
corrects inequalities

riding in a car and wish to read a road sign some distance ahead, the muscles controlling the lens relax and the lens flattens out. If you sit down at a desk and start to read a book, the muscles contract and the lens becomes rounder which gives it the higher power needed for closeup focusing. Changes in the shape of the lens affect the way it bends light.

The space behind the lens is filled with a jellylike substance called the *vitreous humor,* Latin for vital liquid. It helps to keep the eyeball round. Loss of vitreous humor is serious because it cannot be regenerated.

After passing through the vitreous humor, light rays reach the retina. When eyes are functioning perfectly, light rays reflected from something far away or nearby are bent so that they intersect on each retina. In the condition known as nearsightedness (myopia), the light rays from distant objects intersect before they reach the retinas and the image produced is blurry. The cause may be that the eyes are too long from front to back to focus light rays on the retinas. In the condition called farsightedness (hypermetropia), the light rays from nearby objects intersect behind the retinas producing a fuzzy image. The eyes may be too short from front to back for light rays to be bent so that they come to a point on the retina. Eyeglasses correct the bending of light rays to bring them into focus on the retinas.

Another focusing defect is called astigmatism. (The "a"

stands for without, "stigma" means a point). Astigmatism is caused by an irregularity in the curvature of the cornea or of the lens with the result that some light rays from an object are bent differently than others, and therefore, all do not meet at a single point on the retina. Only about one person of every three does not have some degree of astigmatism, but when it is slight it does not interfere with vision. When astigmatism is severe, a person may see the horizontal wires in a screen clearly, but the vertical wires look fuzzy, or the vertical wires may look clear and the horizontal ones fuzzy. Astigmatism is corrected by eyeglasses that compensate for the unevenly curved cornea or lens.

In each retina more than one hundred twenty-six million tiny light-sensitive cells, called rods and cones because they resemble them in form, react to light rays and send signals to the sight center of the brain. Cone cells, which are more important than rod cells in color vision, are concentrated in the part of the retina directly behind the pupil. This area, yellow-orange in color, contains a small depression about the size of a pinhead, called the fovea centralis. It is the area in which our vision is most acute. When looking at something small, we unconsciously move our eyes so that light rays from the small object are focused on the fovea centralis.

The nerve fibres from the rods and cones converge toward the part of the retina called the optic disk. Through it they enter the optic nerve. Then an amazing process occurs. Where the optic nerves from the two eyes meet, the fibres divide into separate tracts. Fibres that originated on the left side of the left eye go into the left optic tract. Nerve fibres from the left side of the right eye cross over and join the fibres from the left eye. Similarly, nerve fibres from the right sides of the two eyes unite in the right optic tract. The brain blends the signals transmitted through the two tracts into one understandable picture.

Every normal eye has a blind spot. Since the optic disk does not contain any light sensitive cells, light rays falling on it are not signaled to the brain. Ordinarily we do not notice our blind spots because their effect is eliminated by a slight movement of the eyes. In addition, one eye usually picks up what the other eye cannot see.

You can learn about the blocking effect of your blind spots by making a simple experiment. On a sheet of paper draw a circle and, about 2½ inches to the right of it, draw a cross. Now hold the paper at arm's length in front of your right eye and close your left eye. You will be able to see both the circle and the cross. Then move the sheet of paper closer to your face. When it is about 12 inches away the cross disappears. Now close your right eye, open your left eye and repeat the experiment. First you will see both the circle and the cross and when you bring the paper closer the circle will disappear. The disappearance of the figures is due to the fact that the light rays from them were focused on the blind spots of the eyes.

By experimenting with this diagram you can learn about the blocking effect of your blind spots.

From *Eye Health* by Colin B. Fryer.

Six muscles move each eye up, down and sideways. Watch when you are talking to someone and you will see that his eyes move almost continually. Rarely are we conscious of the movement of our eyes.

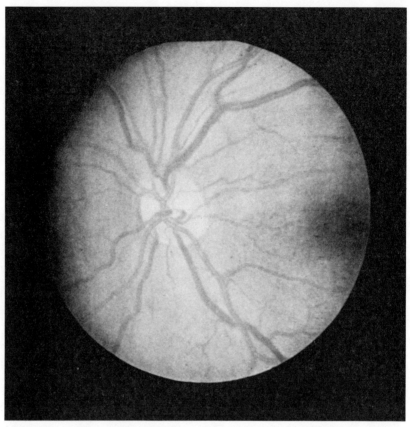

For diagnosing some conditions, a special camera is used to photograph the back of the eye. In this picture, the blood vessels and the optic disk (the blind spot) are clearly shown.

Courtesy of the Polaroid Corporation.

Normally our two eyes move together. If you focus on something to your left, both eyes turn to the left, and if you wish to see something to your right, both eyes turn to the right. If the muscles of the two eyes are not coordinated, the eyes do not turn together. The popular term for this defect is "cross-eyes."

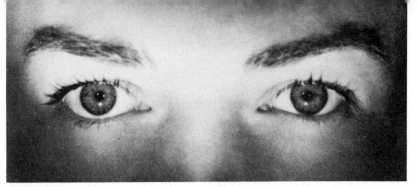

The position of human eyes limits our field of vision.

One eye may be turned in or outward, or one eye may be higher or lower than the other. Such misalignments require treatment not primarily because they look odd, but because they affect vision. When eyes are not in alignment each focuses differently and the brain cannot fuse the images transmitted to it. The result may be double vision: a single pencil appears to be two pencils, a single chair, two chairs. Usually the brain learns to block out one of the images but this may lead to another problem. To tell how far away things are, both eyes must work together. Unless they do, depth perception is defective.

Birds, like this duck hawk, whose eyes are at the sides of its head, can see a much wider area.

Photograph by Jim Yoakum.

Long ago it was believed that cross-eyes would cure themselves, but now treatment is started when children are young. Frequently, special exercises to strengthen an eye's weak or lazy muscles are recommended and "training" glasses are prescribed. In some severe cases an operation on the eye muscles is required.

Even when eyes work as a team, each sees things from a slightly different angle. When looking at any object the right eye sees farther around its right side, the left eye sees more of the left side. From the signals sent from the right and left eyes the brain produces a three dimensional picture with width, height and depth.

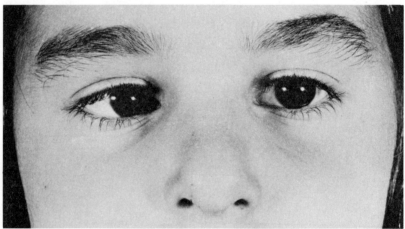

If the muscles of the two eyes are not coordinated, the eyes do not turn together.
Courtesy of the National Society for the Prevention of Blindness.

The position of human eyes in the front of the head limits our field of vision. Birds and some animals, horses for example, whose eyes are on the sides of their heads can see things in a much wider area than we can. Yet our forward looking eyes

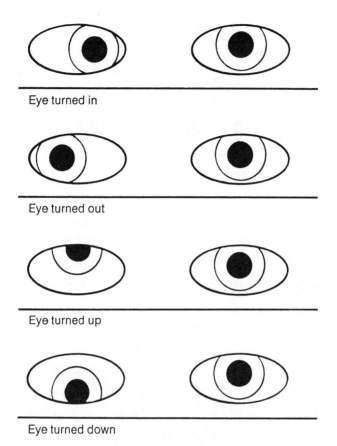

Eye turned in

Eye turned out

Eye turned up

Eye turned down

Different type of defective eye coordination.
Courtesy of the National Society for the Prevention of Blindness.

also have some rear vision. Our eyes can detect objects slightly behind the head. Almost everyone has had the experience of sensing, without hearing footsteps, that someone is approaching from behind. Some authorities say that this is due to the fact that the shadow of the approaching person falls within the narrow sight zone to the side, but somewhat behind, the head of the person being followed.

FOUR

Having Your Eyes Examined

Normally, an eye examination is a painless, interesting experience. The examining may be done by an optometrist or by an ophthalmologist. Both have the title of doctor and are licensed as eye specialists. Optometrists are trained to examine eyes, to evaluate vision problems and to correct them by prescribing eyeglasses and sometimes special exercises. Ophthalmologists are physicians who specialize in all phases of eye care. They too examine eyes, prescribe corrective lenses and for some conditions they may order medicine or perform surgery.

The first time your eyes are examined by an eye physician or an optometrist the procedure is much the same. The doctor starts by asking what vision trouble you have been having. Do your eyes get tired when you read? Do the words look blurry? How well can you see distant things? The questioning includes inquiries about your general health and the eyesight of members of your family, "Does your father or mother wear glasses?" the doctor may ask.

The doctor records your answers on a card which later, after he has added data about your examination, will be filed under your name. Your case history, as the card is called, will provide the doctor with useful information the next time he examines your eyes.

Usually the doctor begins his examination with the Snellen Test for distance vision. It was developed by Dr. Herman Snellen of Utrecht, Holland and was presented at a meeting of eye specialists in 1862. Dr. Snellen designed letters of a special kind called optotypes which, when read at a specified distance, constitute a measure of sharpness of vision, or visual acuity, the term doctors use.

Dr. Snellen made a chart with a large letter *A* on the top line and on the second line smaller letters *G* and *E*. On each of the following five lines the letters were smaller than those on the line above. After testing many people with the chart Dr. Snellen determined which line of letters a person with normal distance vision could read when standing or seated twenty feet from the chart. If, after a Snellen's Test, the doctor says that you have 20/20 vision it means that you are able to read the letters that people with normal distance vision can read at a distance of twenty feet. If, at twenty feet, the last line of letters you can read is the one that people with normal vision can see at forty feet, your distance vision is said to be 20/40 v.a. (visual acuity). The results of a Snellen's Test are always stated as a fraction. The second figure, the denominater, may be less than 20 or more than 20. If it is less, your distance vision is greater than normal, and if the figure is higher than 20 you cannot see as far as a person with normal distance vision.

Since few examining rooms are large enough to give the Snellen Test at a distance of twenty feet, the size of the letters is reduced in proportion to the distance at which they are read. If the distance is ten feet the letters are half the size of what they would be if the distance were twenty feet. However, the result is always stated in terms of twenty feet. Frequently, instead of a Snellen's chart, the doctor flashes the letters on a screen. The use

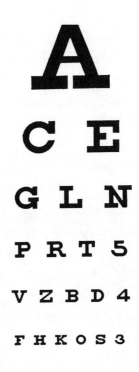

Dr. Snellen's original chart for testing distance vision. The chart was placed twenty feet from the person being tested.

of a screen enables the doctor to vary the letters displayed and thus to eliminate the possibility that a patient has memorized a chart and is not reading it. Since one eye may have sharper vision than the other, each is tested separately.

After the Snellen's Test is completed the doctor may examine the interior of your eyes to determine whether they are healthy or show any abnormalities. To do this he uses a small instrument called an ophthalmoscope. It has a disk at the top containing a number of lenses of varying power, a bulb about one eighth the size of an ordinary flashlight bulb and a reflecting

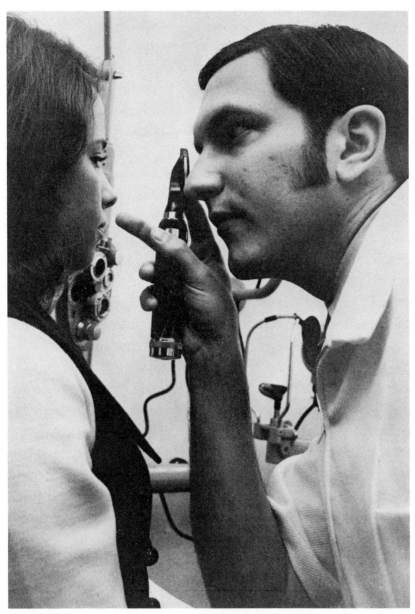

An ophthalmoscope is used to examine the interior of the eyes. The instrument contains a small light which is reflected into the eye.
Courtesy of the American Optometric Association.

prism. Within the instrument's short handle are batteries to which the bulb is connected. The doctor holds the ophthalmoscope to his right eye and close to your right eye. The light from the bulb is cast on the prism from which it is reflected into your eye illuminating the retina. The doctor peers through the sighting hole in the prism and with his index finger selects the lens that gives the sharpest focus on the interior of your eye. He observes the appearance of the retina and the reaction of the pupil to the beam of light from his instrument. A normal pupil becomes smaller when subjected to a bright light. The examination is made primarily to determine the condition of the eye but it also may disclose diseases of the body.

The doctor uses another small instrument, known as a retinoscope, to make precise measurements of how near- or farsighted his patient is. The light in the retinoscope illuminates the retina, and the reflections of the light in the instrument's mirror show how the eye bends, or reflects, light. From an examination with a retinoscope a doctor learns enough to know the power of the corrective lenses that are required.

There is no fixed order in which other tests are made—the procedure varies from doctor to doctor. The next test may be of your field of vision. The simplest way of determining one's ability to see more than what is straight ahead is for the doctor to stand directly in front of you and tell you to focus on his face. Then the doctor says, "Continue to look at my face and tell me the moment you see me moving my fingers." You may think this direction a trifle odd until you see the doctor extend his arms sideways and wiggle his fingers. "You're moving the fingers of both your hands," you report. If side vision appears to be defective, various devices may be used to make exact measurements.

A diagram used to check for astigmatism. Each eye is tested separately with the diagram held at reading distance. Astigmatism is indicated if pie-shaped sections are seen within the concentric circles.
Courtesy of the Better Vision Institute.

Good side vision is important for everyone but it is a requisite for automobile drivers. Defective side vision has caused many collisions.

An instrument that resembles a flashlight may be used to test whether you have normal two-eyed vision, that is, whether your eyes work together as a team. For this test you are given a pair of special glasses to wear. There are four small circles of different colors in the instrument's lens, and when it is illuminated, a person with two-eyed vision can see, through the special glasses, all four colored circles. A person whose eyes do not work as a team can see only two or three colored circles.

If the doctor has found astigmatism in one or both of your eyes, he makes tests to determine the degree to which the astigmatism affects your vision. Most astigmatism is caused by an unevenness in the curvature of the cornea which prevents the focusing of light rays at a single point on the retina. To determine the extent of the astigmatism the doctor may use an instrument that shows a magnified image of the cornea surface. Another test may be made with a diagram composed of concentric circles with spokes extending from the inner to the outermost circle. The patient is asked if all the lines look equally clear or if some look blurry. The patient's response aids the doctor to specify the required correction for astigmatism in the glasses he prescribes.

During the doctor's preliminary questioning he often learns enough about his patient to decide whether a test for defective color vision should be made. This defect is usually inherited and affects more males than females. A chart with a design made up of red and green dots is frequently used for a quick screening test of color vision. The green dots constitute the background, the red dots form numbers. A person who cannot distinguish the numbers has either a red or green color defect and usually is given more tests. One may be a "matching" test which consists of matching a number of chips or yarns of various colors. Fortunately most cases of defective color vision are mild because the condition cannot be remedied.

From his examination the doctor knows whether your vision will be improved by eyeglasses or whether they are not necessary. About one patient in eight does not need glasses.

The doctor relies to some extent on his patient's reactions when determining what lenses will best correct his vision defects. A patient sometimes finds a slightly different correction more comfortable than the one that the doctor's preliminary examination has indicated. The test for determining the most satisfactory lens is made with a Snellen's chart or a projection of the letters. The doctor puts on the patient a masklike frame containing a number of trial lenses, and then moves one that he believes is of the proper power in front of the patient's right eye. The left eye is covered by a shield. "What line on the chart can you read now?" the doctor asks. Then he changes the lens and inquires if it seems better or not as good as the first. More lenses may be tried and one or two that the patient said were good may be tried several times. After the lens trial for one eye is completed, it is repeated for the other eye. The patient's judgment on the lenses he found best is taken into account by the doctor when he prescribes eyeglasses.

Before removing the frame with the trial lenses the doctor tests his patient's near vision. Sometimes a card with lines of type of different sizes is slipped into a holder attached to the frame, or the patient may be handed a printed card or a page and asked how many lines he can read easily. As with the test for distance vision, the near vision of each eye is separately tested. After this test is completed the doctor may remark that you can use the same eyeglasses to correct your far and near seeing defects. Many young people require only one pair of corrective lenses.

At this point the doctor may say that your vision defects can be corrected by spectacles, contact lenses or exercises. A contact lens is a disk that is placed on the cornea and that appears to be part of the eye. Originally all contact lenses were made of glass and were rigid. Today some are made of plastic and are flexible. Practice and skill are required to handle contact lenses. Since they are very tiny, averaging one third of an inch in diameter, great care must be taken that a contact lens is not lost when fitting it on or taking it off the eye. Although contact lenses are much more expensive than spectacles, some people choose them for practical or for cosmetic reasons. For athletes who take part in such active team sports as football or basketball, spectacles may be a handicap that can be eliminated by the use of contact lenses. Some people choose contact lenses because they think that spectacles will detract from their appearance. This, of course, is an old fashioned idea. At present, only a very small percentage of the young people with vision defects use contact lenses.

When the doctor writes out your prescription, he specifies the corrective features to be included in each lens. The prescription for the right eye is designated by the letters OD, the abbreviation for *oculus dexter*, the Latin words for right eye. The left lens is identified by the letters OS, the abbreviation for *oculus sinister*, Latin for left eye.

The power of a lens is given by a figure followed by the letter *D*. The letter means diopter, a unit of measurement of lens power. Other figures and symbols specify the curvature of the lens, and how features of the lens are to be positioned. Prescriptions for eyeglasses are written in technical shorthand which, like ordinary shorthand, makes sense only to those who know how to read it.

If an ophthalmologist has examined your eyes he usually inquires, when handing you his prescription, who will make the spectacles. Eye doctors do not make spectacles but sometimes recommend one or more opticians whom they believe are exact in carrying out a prescription and skilled in fitting spectacles. An optician's business is filling prescriptions for eyeglasses and contact lenses and selling other optical goods.

Doctors of optometry may combine the examination of eyes with the filling of prescriptions for spectacles and contact lenses. However, a patient is always free to decide who will fill the prescription.

FIVE

The Right Spectacles for You

When you go to an optician or to an optometrist to order your first pair of eyeglasses, it is natural that you should look over the frames on display and decide which one you prefer.

However, when you tell the expert who is to fit you with spectacles which frame you have chosen, he may say that it is not the right one for you. A frame must be suitable for the shape and dimensions of your face, he explains. The style of a spectacle frame very positively affects how well you will look when wearing eyeglasses. When a frame is wisely chosen it will accentuate your good features and minimize your poor ones.

No two faces are exactly alike but despite the difference there are two basic types; round and short and long and thin. On a person with a round face, a frame that is narrow from top to bottom in proportion to its length is usually the most becoming. The reverse is true for a person with a long face. For such a person a frame that is wide from top to bottom in proportion to its length is preferable.

Before suggesting a spectacle frame the fitter also takes into consideration the shape and length of your nose. A dark color

41

These highly styled spectacles accentuate the wearer's good features.

plastic frame makes a short nose look even shorter whereas a frame with a dark color upper rim and a lighter color lower rim makes a short nose look longer. Especially if a nose is broad as well as short, a frame with widely curved lower rims looks best and is more comfortable than one with rims that curve close to the nose. For a person with a long, thin nose, a frame with a high bridge makes the nose look longer, a low bridge makes the nose look shorter.

Most stores where spectacles are sold have a narrow table or counter with chairs or stools placed so that the customer and the fitter sit facing each other. While the customer is thinking of style, the fitter is considering technical matters. In addition to making up his mind about the bridge to recommend, he must decide which type pads (the parts of the bridge that fit against the sides of the nose) will be best for his customer. Although pads can be filed down, built up or modified in other ways, it is better if little or no change is required.

An experienced fitter can judge what adjustments of nose pads may be necessary by feeling the structure of your nose with his thumb and forefinger. When a nose is unusually broad or narrow at the top, fitting spectacles so that they will stay in their proper position is difficult but it can be done.

After the fitter has reached a tentative decision as to the best frame for you, he may put it on you and ask if it feels comfortable. No pressure should be felt on the nose during the try-on. When spectacles are worn all day, or even for shorter periods, pads that press into the nose are annoying. If you tell the fitter that the pads feel tight, he may have you try on another frame in which the pads are a little farther apart. Or he may decide that by adjusting the pads of the first frame, it can be made to feel comfortable.

While you try on spectacle frames the fitter checks a number of details. Are your eyes centered in the frame? Do the upper rims of the frame line up with your eyebrows? Are the temples the right length? Some temples are attached near the top rims of the frames and others lower down. Although temples can be bent, the point at which they are attached to the frame limits the adjustment that can be made. The fitter may check the temples from the side as well as from the front to make sure that they are at the right angle and of the right length to grip your head.

The place at which frames are most apt to break is at the

One step in the manufacture of spectacles is cutting the grooves into which the lenses are cemented. In another operation the temples are attached.

Courtesy of the American Optical Corporation
and the Better Vision Institute.

temples, and for this reason they should be attached by sturdy hinges. In a good quality frame the hinges are recessed for their entire length and are anchored with rivets. Metal cores in the temples help to maintain their shape.

Spectacle frames, like clothes, are made in sizes, and it is important to get the right size, not only because the spectacles will look better, but also because they will be more efficient. Every lens has an optical center and in a frame of the right size lining up the optical centers of the lenses with the pupils of the eyes is easier and surer.

To determine how the lenses should be centered, what is known as the pupillary distance (the P.D.) is measured. Although the measurement is usually described as the distance between the pupils, actually an adjustment is made for the way the eyes focus on an object. A small ruler with gradations in millimeters is ordinarily used for the measurement. The fitter holds the ruler just above your eyes with one of his hands and directs you to focus on a pencil that he holds with his other hand, first in front of his right eye and then in front of his left eye. With his right eye closed, the fitter sets the zero mark on the ruler just above the nasal (inner) edge of your right pupil. Then, with his left eye closed and his right eye open, he reads the ruler to get the distance to the outer edge of your left pupil. Although the procedure sounds complicated, it is really quite simple and usually takes less than a minute. Sometimes the P.D. is measured with an instrument based on the same principle as a range finder in a camera.

After a spectacles frame has been decided upon, the fitter may ask if you wish to have the lenses made of glass or of plastic. Such great improvements have been made in plastic lenses that they are considered by some experts to be more desirable than glass. One advantage of plastic lenses is that they weigh about 50 per cent less than glass lenses of the same power. Another advantage is that plastic lenses have a higher resistance to breakage. Also, because plastics have better heat transmission properties than glass, they are less likely to fog. One expert has said, "If plastics had been the traditional material for spectacle lenses, it would be very hard to make the customer change to glass."

However, corrective lenses are more expensive when made of plastic than of glass and they require more careful handling. If you lay down any pair of spectacles on their lenses, you are taking a chance that they may be scratched, but plastic is more susceptible to scratching than is glass. To protect lenses against scratching, put spectacles down on the edge of the frame or slip them into a case. The advice, "On the face or in the case," is easy to remember and wise to follow.

If you order plastic lenses you will probably be told how to clean them. They should be washed with soap and water and while still wet be wiped dry with a soft cloth. If the lenses are dry when they are wiped, the friction will create static electricity with the result that more dirt will collect on the lenses. Because of this problem the optician may impress on you the importance of proper cleaning of plastic lenses. When you choose glass lenses nothing may be mentioned about cleaning, but you should use the soap and water method. Unless lenses are really clean they will not work the way they are supposed to.

Rarely does the man who fits spectacles make them up. Another man, known as an optical mechanic, does whatever grinding is necessary to make a lens conform to the doctor's prescription and to center it correctly in the spectacle frame. It would take a good deal longer, cost more and the lenses would not be as satisfactory if optical mechanics had to start with a piece of optical glass and grind it to meet each individual prescription. Instead they start with a finished, uncut lens. The mechanic has a wide assortment of such lenses in his stock. They are made by manufacturers of optical glass and each lens has a specific curvature and power. For most uncomplicated cases of nearsightedness and farsightedness, all the mechanic need do is to select an

Students at New York City Community College learning to edge lenses to make them fit into selected frames.

Courtesy of the Better Vision Institute.

uncut lens of the power the doctor has specified and grind it down to fit the frame that the customer has selected. To fill a more complicated prescription the mechanic must determine how the lens must be turned and positioned to make it conform to the prescription.

This is so when a lens is to correct for astigmatism (inability of the eye to bend all rays of light from an object so that they come together at a single point on the retina). Such a lens includes what is termed a cylinder. Its optical effect is equalizing the bending of light rays. The doctor specifies in his prescription the direction in which the cylinder is to be turned. It may be in a vertical or horizontal position (or in between) depending on the defect in the curvature of the eye.

All corrective lenses are curved. In the type called a "toric" lens, which formerly was used in most spectacles, the curves in all parts of the lens are not identical. The curves between the top and bottom edges of a toric lens are different from the curves between the side edges. Toric lenses cost less but are not as satisfactory as the type called "corrected curve" lenses. These not only permit good vision through the center of the lens but also minimize distortion when the wearer looks through the top, bottom or sides of the lens.

Manufacturers of optical glass developed corrected curve lenses after making many highly technical experiments and mathematical calculations. Since lenses of different powers require different curves, it was necessary to determine the most effective combination of curves for the front and back surfaces of lenses of each power. Innumerable experiments were conducted to learn how rays of light are bent by various curves. The findings were reduced to complicated mathematical formulas which were applied to the design of corrected curve lenses. As a result of this scientific work we now have lenses that provide real wide-angle vision without any noticeable distortion.

In a finished pair of spectacles it is impossible to tell by ordinary inspection if the lenses are concave (to correct for nearsightedness) or convex (to correct for farsightedness). However, convex lenses are always thicker at the center than at the edges; concave lenses are thicker at the edges than in the center.

When you call for your new spectacles, the fitter asks you to be seated and puts the glasses on you. He looks critically at the way they fit and after moving the frames from side to side and up and down to test how well they stay in place he may say that the temples need adjusting, sometimes to make them snugger and sometimes to ease them. Usually only minor adjustments are needed.

After eyeglasses have been worn for a period of time they may require adjusting, and usually this is done free of charge by the shop that made the spectacles. The shop also keeps your prescription on file and can duplicate a lens that has been broken. Some people take along a copy of their prescription for eyeglasses when they go on vacation so that a replacement of a broken lens can be obtained at an optician's shop in the vacation area. Even if an optician has no prescription to work from, he can tell how to make most lenses by examining the broken one with an instrument called a lensometer. Of course, if you wear glasses all the time it is a good precaution to take an extra pair of spectacles with you.

SIX

Manufacturing Optical Glass

Soon after the Jamestown colony was established in Virginia, Captain John Smith recommended that a "glasshouse" be built. This factory for the production of glass was an immediate success. By 1608, within a year after the factory began operations, it was producing more glass than the colonists needed. The surplus was exported for sale in England. In other colonies, too, the operation of glassmaking factories was profitable, and many of the pieces they made were beautiful. You can see some in museums. But American factories did not make optical glass. Until World War I, most glass of the quality required for spectacles was imported from Europe.

Basically the process of glassmaking is simple and has been known since ancient times. Glass beads made about five thousand years ago have been found in tombs. It is believed that the knowledge of how to make glass developed from the use of glazes on pottery. The glaze mixture was composed largely of sand to which lime, other alkaline materials and coloring were added. After the glaze was applied to a piece of pottery it was placed in an oven and baked at high heat. The heat caused the glaze to liquefy and to coat the pottery with a shiny film.

At some time, either intentionally or accidentally, a potter dropped gobs of his glaze mixture into an oven and produced a new product—glass. One of the first purposes for which it was used was for jewelry. Men learned that while glass was hot it could be kneaded and formed into beads. The glass was not transparent. Transparency was not important until blow pipes were used to form glass into bowls, vases and other decorative pieces.

The technique of glassmaking spread from country to country. Assyrians brought glassmaking to Egypt and by 1500 B.C., Egypt had a well established glass industry. After Rome conquered Egypt, skilled glassmakers were taken to Rome where they continued to work at their trade.

As the centuries passed, craftsmen improved glass by adding different ingredients to the basic recipe. An Englishman,

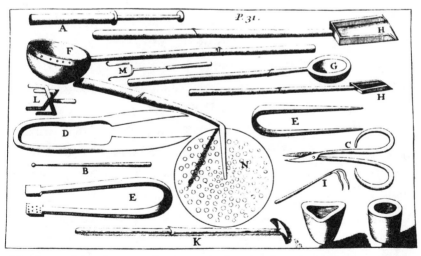

Tools used in the manufacture of glass in the seventeenth century.
Courtesy of the New York Public Library.

Interior of a factory in which glass was manufactured hundreds of years ago.

George Ravenscroft, experimented with the addition of lead and in 1676 produced glass with a high lead content that had great brilliance and clarity. It was also softer than other glass, a characteristic that made cutting and engraving it comparatively easy. First in England, then in other countries, many elaborate cut glass pieces were produced. Another use for glass with a high lead content (from 45 to 65 per cent) is for bifocal lenses.

The manufacture of optical glass is a highly specialized operation and few American companies tackled it while supplies could be conveniently obtained from Europe. During the Civil War, one company that manufactured spectacle frames for which they imported lenses was almost forced out of business because shipments from abroad were disrupted by the war. After this experience, the frame manufacturer decided to make the lenses they needed and established a small optical glass factory.

However, neither this factory, nor others operating in the United States made optical glass of as high quality as European manufacturers. They were the chief source for lenses used in cameras, binoculars, laboratory and military equipment as well as for spectacles. This situation changed after the United States entered World War I. Vast quantities of optical glass needed by the armed forces for gun sights, range finders, submarine periscopes and numerous other purposes had to be produced in American factories. They had to make more, and better, optical glass than they had ever before produced. To fill the wartime orders, glass factories were expanded and techniques refined. When World War I ended, American factories were producing optical glass of really high quality.

Today two methods are used for the manufacture of optical glass. The traditional method of making glass in a clay pot, called a crucible, is used when a comparatively small quantity of glass of a special type (tinted glass, for instance) is to be produced. Crucibles are made of fire clay, a material capable of withstanding extremely high heat. The newer, continuous flow process, which is completely automated, is used for producing optical glass in large quantities.

For both methods the first step is weighing out the ingredients specified in the glass formula. For the continuous flow process some ingredients are used in hundreds of pounds and other ingredients in fractions of an ounce. A big mixer, similar to the concrete mixers often seen at building construction sites, blends the measured ingredients. To them a small quantity of "cullet" is usually added. Cullet is the name given to optical

The first step in making optical glass is weighing out the ingredients specified in the formula. The men wear masks as protection against the inhalation of the chemicals.

The following series courtesy of Bausch & Lomb.

glass that contains defects which make it unusable for lenses. Because cullet has had a prior processing it softens more quickly than the new materials and speeds up their melting.

The pots in which special types of optical glass are made are heated in a furnace for four or five days before they are filled with the mixed ingredients and moved into the melting oven. In this oven the temperature may be as high as 2600° Fahrenheit. The pot is kept in the oven for about twenty-two hours. After the mix liquefies and boils it is stirred to insure that all of the ingredients are blended.

The importance of stirring with a rod made of fire clay was discovered about 1805 by Pierre Louis Guinand, a native of

Switzerland, whose trade was cabinetmaking until he became interested in telescopes. At first he bought optical glass, but it contained so many imperfections that he decided to learn how to make the glass he needed for lenses. He taught himself chemistry and experimented with making glass, usually not more than three or four pounds at a time. Like other glassmakers, Guinand used a wooden rod to stir his mixture, but he could not make the ingredients blend uniformly. The result was that the glass contained air bubbles and specks that Guinand called comets because, like astronomical comets, they had tails. Such imperfections were more serious in glass intended for telescope lenses than for eyeglasses. Guinand cut out chunks of the best glass he produced, but often, after he had completed most of the laborious process of polishing the glass, he saw imperfections in it that made it useless for a lens. Finally, after more than twenty years of making lenses and experimenting with stirrers, Guinand used a stirrer made of fire clay and produced glass that was free of imperfections.

For business reasons, Guinand's technique was kept secret a long time. Until it became known, other glassmakers could not compete with Guinand's company.

A modern stirring rod consists of a water-cooled tube with a clay stirrer at the bottom end. The rods are operated mechanically and the stirring continues for six to seven hours while the glass is slowly cooling.

When an individual batch of glass is being made in a crucible, it is "cooked" until it is about the same consistency as thick molasses. The pot is then removed from the furnace and the glass is poured on a heated iron table. A heavy roller rolls the glass into a sheet, usually about three-eighths of an inch thick. The sheet becomes solid, hard glass almost immediately but it is not yet ready to be molded into lenses. The sheet is moved into another furnace in which the heat is gradually decreased until the glass reaches room temperature. During the manufacturing process samples of the glass are checked periodically, but not until the large sheet has been cut into smaller pieces is the quality of the glass completely tested with special instruments that can detect faults not visible to the naked eye.

Optical glass is rejected if it contains any imperfections. The refractive index of the glass, that is, the speed with which light travels through the glass, must conform to strict standards. Glass that passes all the tests is molded into rough lens blanks which, after a period of reheating and polishing, are then ready for shipment to spectaclemakers.

Hot glass, poured from a crucible to a heated iron table, is rolled into a slab of a thickness suitable for molding into lens blanks.

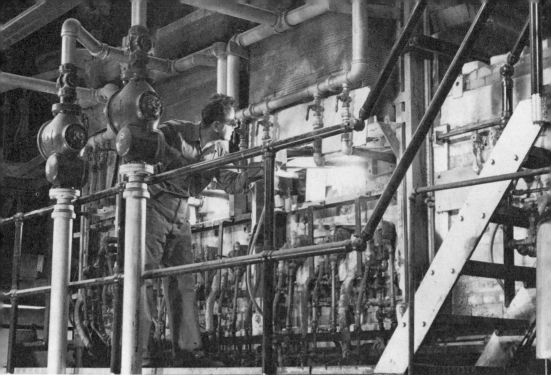

Although the continuous flow process is completely automated, samples of the molten glass are removed at intervals for testing.

Contouring lenses is done in a press. It can be set to produce lenses with different curves.

*Lenses moving out of the oven in which they have been hardened
to make them shatter-resistant.*

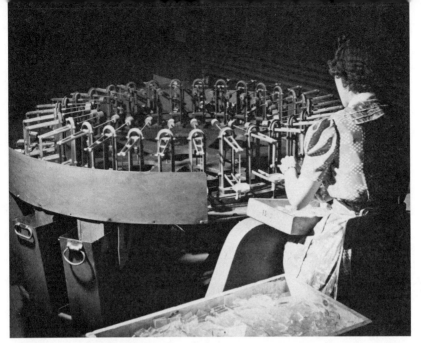

Lens blanks must be of a specified weight. Each blank is weighed on a rotary-type scale.

A machine polishes lenses to optical perfection.

Most glass used for spectacle lenses is produced by the continuous flow process. It is a perfect example of modern automation. The entire process is carried out in a bank of connecting furnaces. Electrical devices regulate the heat and the entire operation. The dry chemicals are fed into the first furnace where they are melted. The molten glass then flows into the second furnace where melting continues. In the third and fourth furnaces the glass is "refined," that is, the undissolved gases are

Many instruments are used to check that lenses conform to established standards, but the final judgment is passed by an experienced inspector.

eliminated. The glass then passes through a machine with automatic shears that snip off gobs of glass which are pressed into rough lens blanks. They drop into a conveyor belt which carries the blanks through another furnace in which they are gradually cooled. Afterwards the lenses are polished.

One of the problems that had to be solved to make the continuous flow process practical was finding the right material for lining the furnaces in which glass is "fined." None of the usual lining materials could withstand the extremely high heat at which these furnaces are operated. After many experiments it was determined that platinum should be used. Platinum, the costly metal that most people associate with jewelry, was selected because it is not affected by molten glass. Since a platinum lining does not break down, there is no possibility that particles of the lining will fall into the glass.

Crown glass, used for spectacle lenses, is usually manufactured by the continuous flow method. Crown glass is composed of about 70 percent sand, 19 percent lime and 16 percent sodium oxide. Only the purest chemicals are used. To improve the quality of optical glass, small quantities of potassium, borax, antimony and arsenic are added to the mix.

As a result of experiments conducted by their chemists, manufacturers of optical glass have developed many special types of glass. For instance, chemists found that the addition of cerium oxide, a comparatively rare metal, produces glass that blocks ultraviolet rays. Other experiments showed that glass to which iron oxide is added absorbs infrared rays.

A company that manufactures optical glass employs many scientists working in different disciplines. Physicists have vastly improved the design of lenses, and chemists have improved the glass of which lenses are made.

SEVEN

Dark Glasses for Sunny Days

Sunglasses are manufactured in such a wide variety of styles that it is a simple matter to find a becoming pair. But how well will they protect your eyes?

Tinted lenses are light filters and can be formulated to screen out a fixed percentage of light. When the Department of Defense drew up specifications for sunglasses to be issued to Army and Navy personnel, it provided that the lenses transmit only 18 percent of the visible light. Sunglasses that meet this requirement are on sale in many stores. There is some disagreement among experts as to precisely how much light sunglasses should pass, but for beach wear, and many other outdoor activities, lenses that pass between 18 to 30 percent are considered satisfactory.

Lenses with greater filtering power are needed to cope with the dazzling brightness in snow country. Some goggles designed for skiers have lenses that filter out 90 percent of the light. The lenses, made of a plastic developed for astronauts, are almost unbreakable. Skiers' goggles may have interchangeable lenses, gray for bright days and yellow for overcast days.

Modern ski goggles can be worn over spectacles. Some goggles have interchangeable lenses for bright and overcast days.

Courtesy of Bausch & Lomb.

As far back as anyone knows, Eskimos wore masks with narrow eye slits to minimize exposure to snow glare. The masks were made of leather, ivory, bone or wood. Eskimos living in different areas used the material that could be obtained most easily. The handmade masks blocked side vision; only what was straight ahead could be seen. When trading posts in the Arctic put on sale factory-made goggles with tinted lenses through which one could see to the side as well as ahead, Eskimos recognized the superiority of the factory-made goggles to the masks they made for themselves. Today, very few Eskimos use handmade masks.

Tinted lenses distort natural colors to a lesser or greater degree. During the first seconds after you put on sunglasses the change in colors is most noticeable but soon the eyes adjust. Gray lenses, sometimes labelled "Neutral Gray" cause the least distortion of color because all the colors in the visible spectrum are absorbed equally.

Sunlight is made up of the colors you see in a rainbow—red, orange, yellow, green, blue and violet. Each color has a different wavelength. Rays of one wavelength give the sensation of blue, rays of another wavelength give the sensation of red. The combined effect of all the rays is white light.

Sometimes it is desirable to block out the light transmitted on one particular wavelength. A yellow lens blocks most of the blue light with the result that contrasts are sharpened. Not only skiers but also boatmen and hunters find yellow lenses helpful on hazy days. However, yellow lenses transmit about 80 percent of the light (as against about 18 percent by neutral gray lenses) and therefore yellow lenses are not appropriate for sunny days.

Generally manufacturers of sunglasses do not supply technical information about how their products can be expected to

An Eskimo wearing a wooden mask with narrow eye slits. Through the slits he could see only what was straight ahead.
Courtesy of the New York Public Library.

Detail of a wooden mask with an upper ledge that provided additional protection against glare. Leather straps held the mask in place.
Courtesy of the Better Vision Institute.

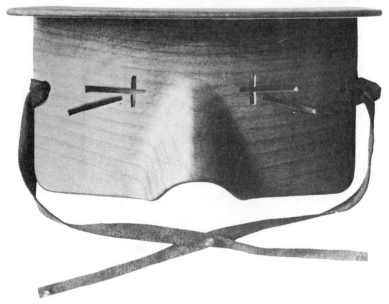

Sunglasses should provide ample coverage above, below and at the sides of the eyes. Lenses should be dark enough so that the eyes cannot be seen clearly when you look in a mirror.

Courtesy of the American Optical Corporation.

perform. People who wear corrective glasses and have sunglasses made to conform to their prescription have an opportunity to discuss with the optician or the optometrist what lenses will be most satisfactory for the intended use. In addition to recommendations as to the filtering power of the lenses and whether they should be made of glass or of plastic, advice is usually given on the shape and size of the frames. Since such information is not available to most buyers of sunglasses, here are some suggestions that will help you to make a wise choice.

First, be certain that the frames are big enough. They should provide ample coverage above, below, and at the sides of the eyes. Big frames for sunglasses are not just a style feature; they give better protection. During the try-on note whether your eyelashes brush against the lenses, an indication that they are too close to your eyes. Sometimes another pair of the same style will fit better, or try a different style. Consider not only which frame you think looks best but also which one feels most comfortable. The glasses should not slip down your nose when you bend over. Some sunglasses have very wide temples, and you may like the way they look but remember that they will obstruct side vision. In some states it is illegal for automobile drivers to wear sunglasses with temples that exceed one-half inch in width.

Often the same style frame is available with lenses of different shades. Although you may prefer a light shade, check by looking in a mirror while trying on the sunglasses whether you can see your eyes quite clearly. If you can, the lenses are too light to protect your eyes.

Look for a label stating that the lenses are "impact resistant." A Federal law now requires that all eyeglass lenses, whether made of glass or of plastic, must be hardened to resist breakage, but for some time to come stores may have old stock that does not meet the Federal requirements. The law specifies how lenses are to be tested. A sample from a batch of lenses is placed in a holder and a steel ball, five-eighths of an inch in diameter, is dropped from a height of fifty inches on the lens. The ball is dropped through a tube and hits the center of the lens. To pass the test the lens must neither crack nor show any visible damage. Enough samples from each batch of lenses are tested to know whether the batch conforms to the specifications for impact resistance. Although such lenses are neither unbreakable nor shatterproof, they do withstand rougher use than untreated glass or plastic lenses.

Some manufacturers are not sufficiently careful in pairing up lenses of exactly the same color and, especially when buying sunglasses sold at a low price, it is wise to compare the color of the lenses. Wearing sunglasses with noticeably mismatched lenses may cause eyestrain.

Lenses that contain tiny imperfections may also be troublesome. Flaws as thin as a hair can be discovered by making a simple test. For it you need an overhead fluorescent light fixture which many stores use for general illumination. Hold the sunglasses under a fluorescent fixture and below your eye level so that you can see the light reflected on the inside of one of the lenses. Then move the sunglasses slowly sideways and watch the reflection of the light as it travels across the lens. If the reflection is wiggly the lens is flawed. In a perfect lens the reflection is seen as a straight line. Repeat the test on the second lens; the first may be perfect and the second imperfect.

Before deciding to buy sunglasses with glass lenses or with

There is a wide variety of styles in sunglasses and it is easy to find a pair that is becoming.

Courtesy of Cool-Ray, Incorporated.

plastic lenses you should know the difference in how these two materials perform. They are equally efficient in filtering the sun's visible rays and the invisible ultraviolet rays that cause sunburn.

However, plastic lenses do not filter out all the invisible infrared (heat) rays, a point emphasized by manufacturers of glass lenses which do block infrared rays. It is possible to make plastics capable of filtering out all infrared rays. In fact, such plastics were manufactured for windows in spacecrafts. However, manufacturers of plastic sunglass lenses do not believe that infrared rays at ground level present a real hazard, and they do not consider that the addition of an infrared filtering material is justified. This opinion appears to be confirmed by the many people who wear sunglasses with plastic lenses and experience no eye trouble.

Plastic is lighter in weight than glass and therefore is more comfortable to wear. Both materials are susceptible to scratching but glass is more prone to breaking and less prone to scratching. The risk of damaging sunglasses is greatest if you put them down on a beach. The lenses may be scratched by the sand or the frames may be overheated and distorted by the sun. To protect your sunglasses slip them into a case when you are not wearing them.

Of the special types of sunglasses, the best known are those with Polaroid lenses. They look like other plastic lenses but they work differently. In addition to filtering light they selectively block some light rays.

The principle of light polarization was known for nearly three hundred years before Polaroid sunglasses were put on sale in the 1930s. They were one of the first products made of an inexpensive polarizing material developed by Edwin R. Land. Prior to Dr. Land's invention, the high cost of polarizing filters had restricted their use. Dr. Land changed this situation and introduced the public to light polarization.

Light from the sun (or from any other source) vibrates as it travels. The vibrations move in all directions except back and forth along the line of travel. When light is polarized all of the vibrations are blocked except those undulating in a single direction. Light may be partially polarized with the result that some of the vibrations are cut out. Partial polarization occurs naturally in many situations where light from an original source is reflected. Some of the light reflected from a smooth surface such as a road or a beach is partially polarized and consists mostly of horizontal vibrations which cause glare.

Polarized sunglass lenses bar the horizontal vibrations. The lenses perform, in effect, as optical slits through which only the vertical rays can pass. Therefore polarized sunglasses are effective in eliminating glare from light reflected from a beach, a body of water or a highway.

Another special kind of sunglasses, known as Photosun,

Light reflected from a beach or a road consists mostly of horizontal vibrations which cause glare. Polarized sunglasses bar the horizontal vibrations.

Courtesy of the Polaroid Corporation.

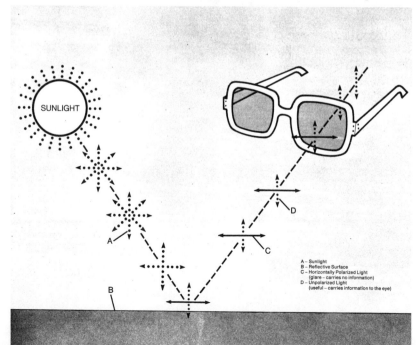

A – Sunlight
B – Reflective Surface
C – Horizontally Polarized Light
   (glare – carries no information)
D – Unpolarized Light
   (useful – carries information to the eye)

Photochromic lenses darken when exposed to sunlight. Indoors the lenses are virtually colorless, but outdoors they become a dark gray.

Courtesy of the Corning Glass Works.

have glass lenses that become darker in color when exposed to sunlight. The brighter the sun shines the darker the gray Photosun lenses become. When darkest, the lenses transmit 20 percent of the visible light which is just about the absorptive power specified by the U.S. Department of Defense. Photosuns darken rapidly, and within one minute after exposure to the sun's ultraviolet rays the lenses reach three-fourths of their maximum filtering power. A person wearing Photosuns is not conscious of the change in their color from light to dark gray, but for an onlooker the process is fascinating to watch. It is faster from light to dark than from dark to light. The lightening takes about an hour and a half. When new, the lenses require exposure to sunlight for several hours to bring them up to their normal performance level, and if not worn for a long period their response will be slower until what the manufacturer calls "excitation" has again taken place.

No one with healthy eyes should wear any sunglasses regularly. It's a fad that may harm the eyes. Overuse of sunglasses makes the eyes sensitive to normal light. Sometimes the eyes become inflamed and in severe cases vision may be affected. The cure for sunglass addiction prescribed by doctors is a gradual decrease in the use of dark glasses until the ex-addict feels no need for them except when out-of-doors in the sun.

Despite the many warnings against wearing sunglasses when driving at night people continue to do so. They probably reason that tinted eyeglasses reduce the glare of headlights but what they do not realize is that sunglasses reduce normal night vision. The time for a driver to wear sunglasses at night is when he stops for a snack at a brightly lighted roadside restaurant. When he is behind the wheel again and removes his sunglasses, his eyes will adjust more quickly to the darkness because they were shielded from the bright light indoors.

EIGHT

The Extension of Vision

Nobody knows who discovered that normal vision can be extended and objects magnified by sighting through two lenses, one in front of the other. This important discovery led first to the building of a telescope and shortly afterwards to the invention of the microscope.

There are several versions of how the telescope came to be developed, but all agree that the start was made with spectacle lenses. According to one account, an apprentice in Hans Lippershey's spectacle shop in Middleburg, Holland was experimenting with lenses and found that when he held one near his eye and another at arm's length, the weathervane on top of the church steeple looked as though it was right in front of him.

When the apprentice told Lippershey about the enlarging effect of focusing through two lenses the spectaclemaker tried it himself and realized that it would not be difficult to construct an instrument capable of making distant objects look nearer. He made one in 1608 by mounting two lenses in a tube.

Some historians think that Lippershey, and not his apprentice, made the first experiment with two lenses. From recorded documents we know that the spectaclemaker said that he himself was the inventor.

Lippershey believed that his instrument would be invaluable for military purposes and wrote about it to the States-General, the governing body of the Netherlands. At the time the Netherlands was fighting for independence from Spain, and Lippershey pointed out that with his spyglass the maneuvering of the Spanish army could be watched and its battle plan learned. Knowing where the enemy planned to attack would give the Dutch a great strategic advantage.

After testing Lippershey's instrument, the States-General offered him an immediate payment of three hundred florins, twice that amount later, and promised to buy two more instruments if the first proved satisfactory.

Lippershey had asked that for thirty years he be granted the sole right to make telescopes and that imitations be prohibited. His request would be considered, he was told, and later might be granted. It never was, possibly because other men claimed that they, and not Lippershey, had invented the telescope. One of the claimants was Zacharias Jansen, who also operated a spectacle shop in Middleburg. There is no proof that substantiates his claim to being the inventor of the telescope, but he is credited with making the first compound microscope, that is, an instrument with more than one system of lenses. Jansen's microscope was much larger than the ones used today. It had a tube a foot and a half long and two inches in diameter.

Because Lippershey was not granted the exclusive right to make telescopes he could not prevent other men from constructing such instruments and soon Dutch "trunks" or "cylinders," as telescopes were then called, were made in many countries.

Galileo Galilei heard in 1609 about Lippershey's invention. Galileo, then a professor of mathematics at the university in

One of the telescopes constructed by Galileo Galilei. The instrument is on display at the Museum of Science in Florence, Italy.
Courtesy of the New York Public Library.

Padua, Italy began to study refraction, the bending of light rays, and then made his first telescope. (Some say that Galileo coined the name for the instrument from the Greek words, *tele*, meaning far off, and *skopein*, to look. Others give credit for the name to Johann Demisiani who was present at a banquet given in honor of Galileo.)

Galileo described his telescope as "a tube in the ends of which I fitted two glass lenses, both plane on one side, but on the other side one spherically convex, and the other concave. Then applying my eye to the concave lens I saw objects satisfactorily large and near, for they appeared one-third of the distance off and nine times larger than when they are seen with the natural eye alone."

With normal vision the apparent size of any object depends on its distance from the observer. If your friend is at the end of the street he looks smaller than when he is standing near you. We are accustomed to this optical effect and take it for granted. A camera, which acts like our eyes, clearly shows how distance affects apparent size. Your friend looks very small on a picture taken when he is at the end of the street. On a second picture

A camera clearly shows how distance affects apparent size. In the first picture the girl is near the end of the street and in the second picture she is nearer the camera and looks much larger.

Photographs by George Roos.

taken when your friend is nearby he fills almost the entire picture.

The light rays from your friend come at a very small angle when he is at a distance and at a much larger angle when he is near. What the lenses of a telescope do is to bend the light rays that bounce off your friend or any object being viewed. This bending of the light rays increases the size of the visual angle and makes a distant object look nearby.

Microscopes also produce an enlarged image by increasing the visual angle of the object being viewed. Most people cannot see anything clearly when it is closer than ten inches from their eyes. Hold this book less than ten inches from your eyes and try to read it. Although you may be able to see the letters it is unlikely that you will be able to make them out. The letters look fuzzy because the eyes cannot bring the light rays from the letters into focus. What a microscope does is to permit the viewer to bring an object close to his eye and to achieve a sharply focused image on his retina. The magnifying power of a microscope depends on how its lenses alter the path of light passing through them. A microscope with a magnifying power of one hundred will show an object one hundred times as large as it would appear without a microscope from ten inches away.

After Galileo began to work with telescopes, he tried using one as a microscope. He started to observe flies and was fascinated by what he saw. On November 11, 1614, he discussed his microscopic observations with a friend and said: "I have seen flies which look as big as lambs and have learned that they are covered over with hair and have very pointed nails by means of which they keep themselves up and walk on glass, although hanging feet upwards, by inserting the point of their nails in the pores of the glass.

Galileo's chief work with telescopes was the study of the heavenly bodies, the sun, moon and stars. To see them more clearly he made a second telescope longer than his first. He used a forty-nine inch tube and for the eyepiece a concave lens that measured one and three-quarter inches in diameter. With this instrument and others that he built, Galileo saw the spots on the sun, and by observing the planets concluded that they revolve around the sun. This conclusion that the planets (including Earth) travel around the sun is contrary to what the Bible states, and Galileo's observations were considered radical and dangerous. He was warned not to say that the sun was the center of our universe but he disregarded the warning. Finally, in 1633, Galileo was ordered to come to Rome where he was tried for opposing the beliefs of the Church. "Guilty" was the verdict of the Court of the Inquisition. To escape torture Galileo confessed that he had erred in his observations. But as he rose from his knees, it is said, he murmured, "Nevertheless the earth does move."

Galileo was permitted to return home but he was kept under constant guard by the Inquisition. Yet he continued with his scientific work and wrote a book in which he summed up his experiments and methods. Before Galileo became blind he instructed a friend in how he ground and polished the lenses for his telescopes and thus what he had learned was passed on.

One fault with Galileo's system of using a single convex lens for his main lens (called the objective) and a single concave lens for his eyepiece was that they gave a comparatively small field of vision. When observing the moon, Galileo could see only about half its diameter. Two other faults were more troublesome. The convex main lens failed to focus all light rays at a single point and therefore did not produce a sharp image. Also, because the rainbow colors that, combined, make white light traveled at different speeds through the lens, the image of a star, or whatever was being viewed, was framed by a colored halo.

Johannes Kepler, one of the scientists with whom Galileo corresponded, believed that the problem of bringing an object into sharp focus could be solved by grinding glass into the same shape as the back of the lens of the human eye. Kepler was the first to state that for a person to see an object distinctly, the light rays from it must come to a sharp focus on the retinas of the eyes. In Kepler's time many people still believed that light was projected from their eyes to an object. In the telescope Kepler designed, the image was seen upside down. Later, another man made a telescope like the one Kepler had designed which, with the addition of a lens called the "erector," showed an object right side up. This addition was useful when telescopes were used for viewing objects on earth.

A Dutch scientist, Christian Huygens, believed that the faults in the Galilean-type telescope could be eliminated by increasing the length of the instrument. In 1655, when he was twenty-six years old, Huygens made a twelve-foot telescope, more than twice the length of any he had seen. With this instrument he discovered the brightest of Saturn's moons. A few months later with a twenty-three-foot telescope, he saw that Saturn was encircled by a ring.

Huygens continued to build longer and longer telescopes: one of one hundred seventy feet was followed by another of two hundred ten feet. Still larger instruments were constructed by other men. The instruments were exceedingly difficult to use and required elaborate apparatus to hoist and lower. The craze

Christian Huygens, the Dutch scientist who made many improvements in telescopes, invented an eyepiece in the seventeenth century that was basically the same as one used today.

Courtesy of the New York Public Library.

for giant length telescopes eventually subsided, but with one of them the English astronomer, James Bradley, measured the diameter of the planet Venus at about 7700 miles.

Among Huygens' great achievements was the development of an eyepiece consisting of two thin convex lenses. It was better than a single-lens eyepiece in two respects; it increased the area that could be viewed and it almost eliminated color distortion. Huygens' basic design is still in use today. He was so highly skilled in making lenses that the Royal Society of England, whose membership included outstanding scientists from many countries, invited Huygens to come to London in 1661 to describe his methods. Work that can be completed in minutes with modern equipment took Huygens hours.

Anton van Leeuwenhoek, the most famous of the early microscopists who like Huygens was Dutch, decided after many experiments that he could work better with an instrument with one lens than with a compound microscope with two lenses. He

Anton van Leeuwenhoek was the most famous of early microscopists. With the powerful lenses he ground for his microscopes he discovered the existence of bacteria.

Courtesy of the New York Public Library.

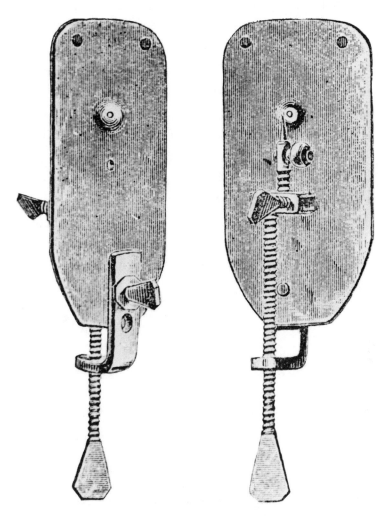

Front and back view of a typical Leeuwenhoek microscope. The screw on the threaded pin was used to adjust the position of the specimen. The microscopes were small, measuring about two inches.
Courtesy of the American Optical Corporation.

was so skilled at grinding lenses that some of them are thought to have been able to magnify objects to five hundred times their actual size. Leeuwenhoek made hundreds of lenses and from them chose the one that enabled him to see most clearly the specimen he was studying. With his most powerful lenses he discovered the existence of bacteria.

Microscopes with a single lens of high power are difficult to work with. Leeuwenhoek's eyesight must have been remarkable for he continued his research with microscopes until shortly before he died at the age of ninety-one. He was self-taught and did not tell anyone how he made his lenses. When Peter the Great, Czar of Russia, came to visit, he was shown a microscope that Leeuwenhoek kept as a display model but not the instruments he used.

Leeuwenhoek reported the results of his observations in long letters to the Royal Society of England. Unlike Huygens he did not go to London to lecture at the meetings of the Society. In 1675, he wrote about "the very little animalcules" he had seen in samples of rainwater.

"I discovered living creatures in rain, which had stood but a few days in a new tub that was painted blue within. This observation provoked me to investigate this water more narrowly. . . .

"When these animalcules bestirred themselves, they sometimes stuck out two little horns, which were continually moved after the fashion of a horse's ears. The part between these little horns was flat, their body else being roundish, save only that it ran somewhat to a point at the hind end; at which pointed end it had a tail near four times as long as the whole body and looking as thick, when viewed through my microscope, as a spider's web. . . . I imagine that ten hundred thousand of these very little animacules are not as big as an ordinary sandgrain."

Leeuwenhoek discovered microbes of other types on leaves, in shellfish, in the intestines of frogs and horses and in mucus scraped from his mouth. His curiosity was endless. He studied the eyes of rabbits, cattle, fishes and birds. His were the first great discoveries made with microscopes.

How Leeuwenhoek would marvel if he could see a modern optical microscope. The excellence of its lenses and the ease with which they can be focused would astonish him. The microscopes we use today were perfected by many men working over a period of hundreds of years.

The same is true of telescopes. In 1663, only sixty-five years after Lippershey invented his telescope, James Gregory, a Scotsman, designed one of a completely different type. All telescopes made before magnified by the use of lenses. This type is known as a refracting telescope. Gregory's design was for a reflecting telescope. In such instruments magnification is achieved by the use of curved mirrors. Gregory's drawing of a reflecting telescope shows two mirrors, one larger than the other, and a lens for the eyepiece. The larger mirror was to collect the light rays entering the tube from the object being viewed and to reflect the rays to the smaller mirror. From it, the rays would pass to the eyepiece. Gregory believed that mirrors would eliminate the distortion caused by the lenses of refracting telescopes.

When he could not obtain mirrors with the curvature and finish he desired, Gregory dropped his idea of constructing a reflecting telescope. Isaac Newton thought the idea had real merit, made some changes in Gregory's design, and in 1668 completed a reflecting telescope. Subsequently, other scientists added improvements and refinements. At the same time as this work was being carried on other men were developing better

An elaborately decorated telescope used in France during the reign of Louis XIV (1643–1715). Louis's rule was marked by lavish display. The palace at Versailles was built for him.

Courtesy of the New York Public Library.

lens systems for refracting telescopes. Today both types are manufactured.

It is impractical to make lenses larger than about forty inches in diameter, and therefore very large astronomical telescopes are of the reflecting type. The biggest mirror yet made for a reflecting telescope measures two hundred inches in diameter. It is made of Pyrex glass similar to that used for cooking utensils.

Many new techniques had to be contrived to produce the giant disk. A dome-shaped oven was constructed to house the mold in which the disk was cast. Because of its shape the structure was nicknamed "the igloo."

The first attempt to cast the mirror failed. Parts of the supporting framework in the mold broke loose and the glass was flawed. As soon as changes in the framework were completed, the engineer in charge of the project cast a second two-hundred-inch mirror.

The procedure was the same as when the first mirror was made. The mold was filled with fiery hot glass, scooped by ladles from the furnace in which it had been melted. Each ladle, moving on an overhead monorail track, contained seven hundred fifty pounds of melted glass which had been heated to a temperature of 2700 degrees Fahrenheit. It took about six hours to fill the mold. It was kept in the igloo oven for a short period, and then the mold was lowered into another oven, called the annealing oven. In this oven the temperature was reduced by seven-tenths of a degree each day. When, at the end of ten months, the twenty-ton disk was moved from the annealing oven, every inch of the glass was examined for imperfections. There were none.

The final polishing of the two-hundred-inch mirror. The cellular structure of the mirror is clearly seen.

Courtesy of the Mount Wilson and Palomar Observatories.

Moonlight view of the Mount Palomar observatory with the shutter open and the telescope in use.

Courtesy of the Mount Wilson and Palomar Observatories.

The next step was the grinding of the disk to the desired curvature. Five tons of glass were removed during this process. Grinding and polishing the mirror took four years.

While work on the mirror proceeded, the rest of the telescope was built. The forty-four-foot rigid tube was made of welded steel and was finished in a year. World War II interrupted the work and not until 1948, fourteen years after the giant mirror was cast, was the reflecting telescope officially put into service in the observatory at Mount Palomar, California. The telescope has extended man's view of the heavens to twelve billion light-years from the earth. (One light-year is about equal to 5,880,000,000,000 miles.) With this instrument, scientists are probing outer space and learning about the birth and death of stars, the age of the sun and how the universe was formed.

NINE

Save Your Eyes

Many people wear goggles to protect their eyes against unusual hazards. The astronauts who walked on the moon wore goggles. In most states employers are required by law to supply goggles to workers who are exposed to the spattering of chemicals, sparks or other dangers to the eyes. The use of goggles is recommended in school and home workshops.

Spectacles are not a substitute for goggles, but there are times when a person who wears eyeglasses is better off than one who does not. On windy days, for example, spectacles shield the eyes from the specks of dirt that are blown around. And during heavy rainstorms, spectacles prevent the rain from directly striking the eyes. Spectacles supplement the eyes' natural defenses.

The eyeball is embedded in a bony cavity called the eyesocket and its outer rim absorbs most blows before they reach the eye. The upper part of the rim is under your eyebrow and the lower part is under the skin directly below your eye.

Eyelids are really efficient protective covers. They can either be shut tight or held partially open. If you are looking into glaring light, the headlights of an approaching car for example, you lower your eyelids enough to block out some of the glare. This movement of the eyelids is instinctive. You consciously close your eyelids when you decide to go to sleep.

The hairs with which eyelids are fringed serve as screens that catch most dirt particles before they can enter the eyes. The hairs on the upper lids are longer than those on the lower lids and curl upward; the lower eyelashes point downward. The length of the upper lashes and the direction in which they curl adds to the beauty of eyes, but Mother Nature was not concerned with appearances when eyelashes were evolving. They turn the way they do so that eyelashes will not interlock when the eyelids are closed. Lashes are lubricated by an oily fluid. You can see, between the roots of the lashes, the tiny openings through which the oily fluid is discharged.

The fluid also lubricates the membrane that lines the lids. The conjunctiva, as the lining is called, connects the lid to the front of the eyeball. While looking in a mirror pull down the lower lid of one of your eyes, and you will see the moist conjunctiva. It is not very sensitive but don't touch it. Even though you think your fingers are clean there may be bacteria on them.

The openings of the tear glands at the outer corners of the eyes are hidden from view. The salty fluid we call tears cleans the eyes and keeps them moist. Eyes are always covered by a thin film of tears. Every time you blink, which normally is every two and a half seconds, the upper and lower lids mop the eyes with the tear fluid. Some of it evaporates and some collects in the inner corners of the eyes where there are ducts which carry the fluid into the nose. Ordinarily the discharge is not noticeable but when, for one of a number of reasons, a greater than usual quantity of fluid is produced, the ducts cannot carry all of it away and tears flood out of the eyes and run down your cheeks.

Excessive tearing often occurs when a speck of dirt gets into an eye. The tears sometimes wash away the speck. If they do not, the first place to look for the speck is in the lining of the lids. According to the First Aid Manual published by the American Red Cross this is what a member of your family, or a friend, should do:

1. Pull down the lower lid to determine whether or not the object lies on the inner surface.

2. If the object lies on the inner surface, lift it gently with the corner of a clean handkerchief or paper tissue. Never use dry cotton around the eye.

3. If the object has not been located, it may be lodged beneath the upper lid.

a. While the victim looks down, grasp the lashes of the upper lid gently.

b. Pull the upper lid forward and down over the lower lid. Tears may dislodge the foreign object.

c. If the foreign object has not been dislodged, depress the victim's upper lid with a matchstick or similar object placed horizontally on the top of the cartilage [which is underneath the eyelid] and evert [turn it inside out] the lid, by pulling upward on the lashes against the matchstick. Lift off the foreign object with the corner of a clean handkerchief and replace the lid by pulling downward gently on the lashes.

d. Flush the eye with water.

c. If the object is still not removed and is suspected to be embedded, apply a dry, protective dressing and consult a physician.

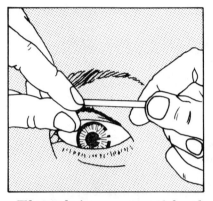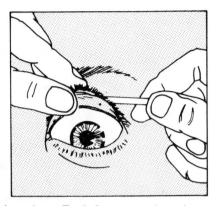

The technique suggested by the American Red Cross for locating and removing a speck of dirt from the lining of the upper eyelid is to turn it inside out by pulling the lid gently upward against a wooden matchstick.

From the American Red Cross, *Standard First Aid and Personal Safety.*

If the speck is on the sclera (the white of the eye) you may be able to dislodge the particle by washing the eye.

You do not need to buy a prepared eyewash. A homemade solution of one teaspoonful of salt and one pint of water (which is about the same composition as tears) is recommended by eye doctors. The solution should be boiled and cooled before it is used. It can be made in advance and kept in the medicine cabinet. A dropper that can be purchased at any drug store is handy for dropping the solution into the eye. Or the solution can be poured into the eye from the spout of a teapot or of a measuring cup. Whichever you use, hold it about an inch from the eye and do not touch the eye itself. Many doctors advise against the use of an eye cup, a small container shaped to fit over the eye and held in place by suction. Unless an eye cup is properly sterilized, it may cause an infection. If flushing the eye does not budge the speck, try touching it lightly with a corner of a clean handkerchief moistened with the eyewash solution. Do not exert any pressure. If at first you don't succeed, see a doctor.

Professional help should be sought promptly if a speck settles on a cornea. Many airborne specks have jagged edges that may scratch or cut the eye. An amateur should never attempt to remove a speck from a cornea.

Inflammation of the eyelids is another condition about which a doctor should be consulted. The redness and swelling may be caused by an infection that can be cured quickly with proper treatment. One commonsense precaution against infection is never to rub your eyes. To drive this point home one eye specialist advises that if you feel you must rub your eyes use your elbows. What he really meant is never rub your eyes.

The most common infection of the eyelids is called a sty. It is a pimple, or small abcess, on the edge of the lid. Sties are caused by germs, and although the infection is not usually serious it can spread from one part of the lid to another. The safest course, if a sty develops, is to ask a doctor what to do.

The condition called "pink eye" is an infection of the lining of the lid and of the white of the eye. Usually the eye is red, not pink. The infection causes dryness and burning. After a time a secretion composed of pus, mucus or a combination of both forms during the night on the eyelashes and makes them stick together. Pinkeye is highly contagious and should be treated promptly. Ordinarily the infection responds quickly to treatment.

People may complain of eye strain whether or not they wear spectacles. For a spectacle wearer the cause may be nothing more than that his spectacle frames are slightly bent, and as a result, the lenses are not in proper alignment with his eyes. Or an eye examination may disclose that a change in lenses is required. Everyone should have his eyes examined if they frequently feel strained. However, the possibility that eye strain may be a psychological reaction should not be neglected. As one eye specialist has pointed out, a boy who can read for hours without complaining of eye strain when he is interested in what he is reading may complain that his eyes are tired soon after he has started some assigned reading that bores him.

Often the cause of eye strain is improper light, a condition that may exist during the day as well as at night. During the day, if you sit facing a window while reading or writing, you are subjecting your eyes to glare from the natural light. You can avoid glare by sitting with your back to the window.

At night it is important to eliminate sharp contrasts of light. A desk lamp used as the only source of light in a room does not provide enough uniform illumination. Other lamps, wall or ceiling fixtures are needed to supplement the localized light of the desk lamp. When only one area in a room is illuminated, eyes must continuously adjust for changes in the intensity of the light. Making these adjustments tires the eyes.

Lighting experts say that a desk lamp should be placed about fifteen inches from the center of your work area. Whether the lamp should be to your right or left depends on whether you are right- or left-handed. The lamp should be on the opposite side to the hand you use so that it will not cast shadows on the book you are reading or the paper you write on. The bottom of the lamp shade should be at eye level.

The idea that reading in bed causes eye strain probably originated because the average bedside lamp does not give enough light. You need as much light when reading in bed as when you are sitting at your desk.

The correct position for a desk lamp is fifteen inches from the center of the work area. The lamp should be opposite the hand you use.
Courtesy of the Better Light Better Sight Bureau.

In the early days of television many people worried about its effect on the eyes, but with the passing of time doctors have concluded that TV does not cause any organic damage to the eyes. However, there are a few commonsense rules that should be observed.

1. Tune the set carefully to get a sharp picture. A fuzzy picture tires the eyes.

2. Don't watch television in a dark room. There should be an overhead light or a light in back of you to reduce the contrast between the brightness of the screen and other parts of the room.

3. Sit directly in front of the screen. Viewing TV from a sharp angle for a long period is apt to cause eye strain. When children watch television they should not sit on the floor and look up at the screen. The set should be at their eye level.

4. Keep your distance from the screen. When the size of the room permits, watch television from a distance of ten feet or more. If you must get close up to the screen to see the program your eyes should be examined. You may need eyeglasses or a change of lenses.

Television, fast moving vehicles and other demands on vision made by our modern world challenge eyes as they never were challenged in earlier times. But it is probable that people see better today than ever before. For more people wear spectacles and spectacles are more efficient than they ever were.

Index